"Johannesburg"
"Key to the Highway"

"Grenada"
"Eyesight to
the Blind"

Hansen

June 28, 1993
919 N. LaSalle
Chicago

Johannesburg & Other Poems

Souders Bottoms — p. 32
Grenada p. 59
blue — origin of word as sad?
fitness Test for the soul — blues — p. 81
is blues focusing on troubles?
griots? p. 96

Phoinolory
— tell us about
this poem
explicate it —

toi toi?

Other titles by Sterling Plumpp
The Mojo Hands Call, I Must Go
Blues, The Story Always Untold
Von Freeman
Somehow We Survive (ed.)
Black Rituals

Johannesburg & Other Poems

By Sterling Plumpp

Another Chicago Press

Copyright © 1993 by Sterling Plumpp

All rights reserved

Published by Another Chicago Press,
PO Box 11223, Chicago IL 60616

The author wishes to thank the following publications in which some of the poems in this volume have previously appeared: *Another Chicago Magazine, Black World, Blues Revue Quarterly, Chicago-Defender, Chicago Music Magazine, Congressional Record, Flair, Living Blues, Mississippi Black Poets, Open Places, Original Chicago Blues Annual, Popular Music and Society, Soho V* (London), *TriQuarterly,* and *TwoTone* (Johannesburg).

Special Thanks to Bernina Harris, whithout whose prowess on the computer this manuscript would have expired in chaos; *The New Nation*, without whose gracious invitation to visit South Africa and participate in the New Nation Writer Conference a part of me would have gone unexplored; and Harriet Nzinga Plumpp, without whose love and quest for excellence to fuel my enthusiasm, it would have surely gone dry.

Library of Congress..........

ISBN: 0-929968-33-6

Distributed exclusively by The Talman Company, 131 Spring St., #201E-N, New York, NY 10012

0 1 2 3 4 5 6 7 8 9

To
Claudette Crystal Miles-White
my daughter
who
commented:
"you forget about your family
and
dedicate books
to
women."
Maybe
she
does not know
why.

Birthright

My Lord said I was born
in a shotgun house
cause I got buckshot
in my heart. Said He
ain't no big house God.
He born in a log cabin
with holes in the walls;
his telephone line to
heaven. Where he dialed
with His voice, open air
the celestial line. I
come from a Third Generation of
moaners. He said some songs
for bended knees; some for
kicking ass. That's why
He 'lowed me to pen the
blues

Metamorphosis

Worst Than the Blues My Daddy Had

I got troubles hurting way, way down inside so bad
I got troubles hurting way, way down inside so bad
I got this something worst than the blues my daddy had

I get up early in the morning think about the roads I've been
I get up early in the morning think about the roads I've been
I try to forget all my problems, seem like my pain will never end

I came to Chicago then I got me a good factory job
I came to Chicago then I got me a good factory job
I left Mississippi when all the booweavils formed a mob

You know they took most of my cotton before I got to gin
You know they took most of my cotton before I got to gin
Then along come Mister Charlie to get the rest with his pen

I got troubles hurting way, way down inside so bad
I got troubles hurting way, way down inside so bad
I got this something worst than the blues my daddy had

They made me work, pray, and have a little hope
They made me work, pray, and have a little hope
Then told him if he didn't like it he'd swing from a rope

They shamed my mother and then handed her over to
   Miss Ann
They shamed my mother and then handed her over to
   Miss Ann
Saying things work out fine under the plantation plan

I got to this city, my grandmomma is shot in the face
I got to this city, my grandmomma is shot in the face
They say they wouldn't have if she wasn't in the robbing
   place

Kids in gangs killing one another all around
Kids in gangs killing one another all around
I pray but no angel of mercy will come down.

I got troubles hurting way, way down inside so bad
I got troubles hurting way, way down inside so bad
I got this something worst than the blues my daddy had.

Turf Song

I speak no polite
language. For slave
cabins teach in codes.
And I was born
one step
from dirt floors.
My shot
gunned entry/jarred articulate
modulation. So I
fell under
the house. Slapped a snake side hisses,
choked a frog's
croaks, and mimed
a rooster/praying
dawn. Growed up/through
cracks in screams, playing
hide under shouts: last
night, the night before/a
Bugga Man and griot/at
my door. I rambled
around moans. Opened
up/by the count of
ten/but a sweet little thing
slid right in/all hid?

I speak undeclared dry
bones' war; connecting
skirmishes a/long edges of
speech. Banter of shovels

memorializing fallen comrades/with
heaved salutes of
mud. Ruptured chords of
voiceless drums/I speak.
Scattered over three
continents. Music/conscience
stomped its toe on/I speak.
Sounds I think/I heard
before I was born.

My history's missing in
sides/I speak. Punctured guts
spilling laws over
commandeered enlightment.
Smashed in/to civilized
splinters, I bang manners
in the head/with a rolling
pin/all hid? Tramped-down
pleas/I speak. Cramped-bile-
rot, ship-hole-puke,
maggoty/dreams-aroma,
burnt-flesh-powder/I speak.
The cellar-swallowing-
drooped-eyed-whispers.
Hind my little shack/where
I steal my last name back.

Ground cracked beneath/I
speak. Make any move/earth
quakes. A situation blues of
death: weeping behind veiled
souls. Rumbling hysteria/I
speak. I got the empty

tongue blues/I cannot
say no/thing but feelings.
I am a woe man/using cries
as buildings. To live a
way. From a hammer. Time raps
against my brains. I speak dis
shoveled logic; a foul utterance.
I got. When Bukka/let just a
little bit of his history creep in
to an/other change of clothes.
And I broke outta Parch
man. I could never
beg. Cause I was
nursed by mumba peg.

Hurt me a little more, I was hurting
all the time.
Hurt me a little more, I was hurting
all the time.
Put more troubles on my troubles
and I ain't never got a dime.

Hard times before me bad, fifty
miles deep.
Hard times before me bad, fifty
miles deep.
Troubles I got so strong, Lord knows,
they put me to sleep.

I sing so lonely cause my soul
on fire.
I song so lonely cause my soul
on fire.

I can't end a song, my own words
make me die.

I speak no polite language; no
unmartyred lyrics.

Prayer For a Bluesman

(for my grandfather)

A census of tears and
a thermometer: a legacy.
Windows
open.
The old
man's harvest, parched
in
his eyes.
Laughter as a fringe
benefit of
his endurance.
A world of parity

in clasped hands.

A bid
whist tournament:
chitlins
on cornbread.
As consolation
prize. Memory.

Aunt

You
beat the spreading
adder coiled
in a little boy's
fears.
Crushed
its head and
the nephew
jerked
the quivering thing
from his mind.
And
you
mended his skin
with two bits of
the good stuff
you
say
when
you don't

say

Lens for Black Eyes

Folder of darkness into
spirals. Slow blues,
optometrist of consciousness.
Lens for black eyes
in the woman in cells of
my being. A paroler
in overalls and rubber
boots. Wader through
daughters of mud. A
weaver of long nights.
Folder of darkness into spirals.
Blessed with screams;
offered as candles of
loneliness. Lit by
touches from a rotunda of
admissions to selves a
lone. Where a metal
rainbow rusts in memory.

Blues Woman

When
I
sell you wolf
tickets
you ain't got enough heart
to buy'em.
And
you
ain't got enough ass
to put'em
on credit.

You
hum from your bending.
To deal
hopes from shadows.

I
hear
you
from outside of
the outside.
An
ace out
side the deck.

A
delta of fertility
in my mother's dawns.

A
kingdom of dust
for her evenings.
Outside
the outside of
the outside.

Her
laughter and
two sons
as a teen
ager.

Blues Woman.

Outside
the outside of
the outside.

Tales
mingle with bruises
on decisions
in your puffy eyes.
A
man's gift.
Anthracite
of mis-aimed Something

polling

a vision
it
does not grow.

Pain
is an annuity
you
invest in
daily.

Interest
a
name

you

call
your song.

Blues Woman.

Outside
the outside of
the outside.

Shadow

      America can
not see
its face. Does
not give a
wards to a poet.

      (For singing.

My father's
    pain. His vision
from dust and
Ernest Robinson's quarters.
His big black
frame. Bold
to affirm his will.
Master of his lodge;
deacon of his words.
They said
he chunked rocks
and they hummed
back
his language
his ancestral blues.
Torn sleeves of
his spirits are mysteries
I peruse with a/pen and
my own vinegar barks.

A
merica does not
want to hear.

Ghosts he threw punches
at/cry their anti
septic beggings
to his clapping in
side his soul.
(A poet is not
encouraged to see.

They put the
winds a
round him
on trial.

                             (For crying.)
My father's mangled dreams.
Sedition: they claim in
writs and
other tongues of chains.
I heard the
wind testify. Its
bloody evocations made
a reddish sky patch.
And I ran to catch it
but my father's voice
fell headless
to earth. It
touched my hands
and I swore to write its
history.

tells her: treat me any
way/you want to. He pours
back the ink

Blues From the Bloodseed

Born be/hind chants of
hands/panting against long
hours/remembered terrors.
ilved be/hind chances and
greed/a long ways from where
I begin. Shadows woke
me in/to mudcaked memories;
voices bubbling through grime
to plant. Shadows woke me
in/to Mississippi/a million
miles from spirits of my
desire. A million miles
to whips of fire. The blues
burning in my eye.

I got the jimson weed blues
and I can't see right. A million
in Dixie/whets my soul's appetite.
Clinton and winter/clamping fog
over hearts. Sixteen sections.
I break 'muda grass wound round
my future/run to RTA and electric
lines/at thirteen. Bro/me the only
boys to roam woods/plow and saw logs.
hear songs of farming men bounce off
saws and bang against oaks, fall in/to

wet leaves. Momma and Poppa sing
thelordwillmakeawaysomehow blues.
theeverythingwillbealright blues.
theithankthelord blues.

seem like/world wanna catch me/
step in every step I take fore
I git out it. Plowing/days
so long and sun sticks his hot
tongue down in my spine. Each
step on the devil's fork/coming
from below/tells me to slow
down. Sweat, mosquito bites, cut
foots/stop at debts and long
winters 'head. I want my heart
smile on day/and I lives. Each
second to its flower. Each minute
to its fruit. Each hour to its
harvest. Each to its full cribs
of corn. Space/I gotta have and
time I gotta find.

"Dude" I hear. "You al/ways
moving like a stream. Just
like water after a storm."
Blues/I say is my life on wheels
and I travels most all the
time. Women in Mississippi.
Good whiskey in Chicago. I
remember loneliness. Fear.
I saw my/self. Stiff. Laid
in a hole/ten miles from no/where.
Buried be/hind light. Lived be/hind

debts and threats. Buried be/hind
silence and time. Every dog
gone thing I seen/somewhere mocking
my hands bound in darkness.
I chose path of will: took my
little rags/hit the road and
lived.

Blues/I say is time and
silence. Planted in/side
my bones. Old folks spewing
lightning from eyes/ten devils
couldn't look in. The crazy
man's blues/I hear in Willie
Johnson. Say a purple monster
with three legs/lay cross the
road/he couldn't pass. Fell
a/sleep and monster gone/when
he woke up. Lying Fred Taylor
say/when he dying/he could hear
death's foot/steps. He there,
eyes, half-closed whispering
with a cackle in his throat and
mad. Cause death put his foot
on his brand new shoes by the bed.

The crazy man's blues/I got
in going and going. Never
finding time's floor. Going
and going. Down and a/round.
Say/the blues al/ways got me
bound. Chicago/no/thing but
Mississippi with concrete.

Spending money/Sun/day clothes
every day. Chicago/long ways
from memories and silence down
in dirt. Home/with a whip in
its hands. Mississippi/land
of king cotton and my daddy's
unsuccessful plans. Ground
crying with time and silence/
and time for me. Silence and time
and me planted/in each other.
Mississippi/home with a whip

Mississippi/my passage
and time and silence. Blood
line sifted/through mud. Red
clay blues/calling for its
hard/time dues. Birth place
of my time/handed down in twine
whispered under owl's cries.
My passing/from pleated backs/
to seats/up front in memory.
Muddy water/in foot/steps of
a nation. My time and song
planted in silence. I rise
in its ditches/crying for
roads/whisked a/way by floods.

I say/hey hey what kind of
place/can Mississippi be?
Seem like every dream
I get/Mississippi wanna
take a/way from me. Mississippi.
Mississippi blues/all I know.

Red/clay soil where my hopes
must grow. Blood/line sifted/
through cracks in river bottoms.

I rise from night/mares and
stallions. Riding the wind/
spurring minutes with songs
in my eyes. With my red/clay
blues/calling eternity to
my side.

Mississippi. Mississippi blues/all
I know. Place/a let back top
took my baby a/way for sure.
I say/hey hey what kinda place/
can Mississippi be? Put my soul
in a cotton/field/forced my name
go under the third degree. Black
jacks knocks. Teeth of ropes
barking hind a moon. Watching
place I may die soon. Blood/line
and memory. Time and silence
bursting outta my voice. Legacy
some/where in a/nother time.

Heard my grand/daddy say:
swamps and snakes no reason
stop plowing in bottom.
Them voices I hears every/
time plow bite ground. Loud
'nough, sad 'nough, mad 'nough/
make me cry, wanna kill. Plow a
row one day/whole choir stood up

29

in muddy robes/cussing the wind
through dirty slobber. Singing
the blues with spit and mud.
I say/hey hey what kinda place/
can Mississippi be? Heard night
crying/silence done spoke. Medgar
gone like many with necks/broke.
Heard earth trembling/time
done spoke. Change done come/
giving mores a big poke. Mississippi.
Mississippi blues/all I know.

They gave me their blues/then
sued me for more. I say/hey hey
what kinda place/can Mississippi
be. Seem like/every freedom
I get/Mississippi memory
want take from me. Passage in
side/where I plant and bloodseeds
grow. Red/clay fertility be/hind
tall grass. Red clay blues/leaping
from skin. Taking a/way its enforced
as a sin. Red/clay blues/time
and silence wound in my days.
Years/boys say history crumble
like rotten wood/and attitudes
blossom like honey/suckles on
fences. Little Rock, Montgomery,
Greensboro. Time with history
by its heels/shaking dust
from its pockets. Changes done
come giving mores a poke. Medgar
gone/wearing struggle's yoke.

Mississippi. Mississippi blues/
all I know. I inherited them
cause I was black and poor. Call
like a freight train/but cries
don't reach no/body's door. I say/hey
hey what kinda place/can Mississippi
be? Wanna put its fingers
on every/thing I see. The women/
I love so well. My peoples's lives
I was born to tell. My folks' lives
I was born to tell.

Sanders Bottoms

(for Mattie Emmanuel)

1

Home/land the landless
'herited. Plots of the
future/down behind generations.
Heir property/locked in blood.
Land/nobody wants to know.
Winding acres of unsung blues.
Land/spirituals come up
in. Pasture of suffering/
home of yearning. Twisting
miles in my soul. Like rusted
wire/tangled round a sampling.

2

Plodding for food/like man;
gallon of blackberries and
a bucket of peas or beans
clutching each hand. Balanced
on my head a basket/of okra
or something to sell or
swap. Reckly after sunrise/
setting out: not coming back
til money or food is gotten.
Remembering/remembering Auntie
done told me a thousand times;
never come back with nothing.
Remembering/her pushing a

straw hat/down almost over
my eyes/saying: "Now, git."

    3
A corner/all I ever got.
Do-mes hanging me out
like clothes on a line.
My days/scattered before me
like wild geese without
a leader. And my prayers
calling them together again.

My life/a string tied
to every need in the house.
Backward I go/for my road
is always up a muddy hill.
I am throwed away/nobody
never gives a child away.

    4
Remember Momma/saying
she was marrying. And the man
didn't want me and Riley.
Only wanted his chilluns
by her. Remember how
I looked out and saw a
ought/and the ought was me.

Something cut the rope/pulling
my dreams from a pit. And I
felt waterless tears/falling
into years.

5

Been believing/ever since
on a mourner's bench/and I asked.
And He done answered my prayers.
Some git they 'ligion with
they tongues and heads/got mine
with my heart believing.

Nine years old/and down on
my knees wanting salvation.
Not knowing what saved was/
but I asked Him; no, I believe,
sweat had bathed me and only
silence come out when I open
my mouth. But I said: "Lord,
I accept You but I need a sign."
Then one night/I went outside.
Saw five stars all hugging and
I asked Him to separate them/as
a sign.

  I shut my eyes/when I
opened them/He done stretched distance
'tween them blinking lights/way up
yonder in the sky.

  I was His/and His presence
reached down and touched me/yes it
  did

6

O remembering/Riley let

nobody put knots on him.
Heard the Leamus boys saying
they gon git him/gon git him
in the woods; kill him. He beat
them up/and Auntie hear it too/
and make Riley/pack up his
sack/Take him to Old Man
Whitley/a white man/give him
away again. Then Riley/gone
and Mister Whitley say last
time/he seed him/he walking along
banks of the pond.
Then/I felt darkness crowding
my eyes/like they say death
pulls down your eyelids and
you can't see in the broad
daylight. Riley/gone and maybe
I'll be gone soon.

   But He lifted
the night away and though my body wept/
joy led me through the days.

   7
I grew/like a trim sapling
and kept serving them/

motherless

   though I minded
my aunt. Soon the Leamus boys/start
messing with me. Tell Auntie/Mr. Leamus

say no blood 'tween me and
his boys.

Don't care what happen to me.

The ground moved
from under me/Auntie tell me

"Stop what you doing
pack your little rags
I'm taking you back
to your momma:

   don't want no Leamuses
   in my family."

Sometimes/you wonder. I looked
out/all I seen was wilderness.
Not one ray
was in my life; started going
to Mound Hood. That's how I met
Victor/he was ugly and evil.
But he was good
to me/all forty-two years;
he was good
to me and never let
nobody mistreat me.

When I met him/Momma was glad
she could marry me off. Then a
little clearing appeared out
in the wilderness.

8

Then/I was big, kinda like one
small vine wanting to climb
a pole/in a big field. Each time

I got big/another vine climb
a pole. On and on/til seven vines
climb up; then it seem like
a whole forest. Mothering them/
through colds, mumps, and measles;
take blood from my heart.

I look
out/and the wilderness is gone.

All seven/my chilluns grow
and Victor make me/stay home.
Clean up
wash and iron
work my flower yard
and plant my garden.

Farming/a
see-saw and booweavils and droughts
up
more times than good crops.
We make do, somehow; keep going,
somehow; and going some more.

9

Afterwhile/grandchilluns come
till seven reached. Victor them
in fields/stay out there; hot sun

boiling down. Stay out there/plowing
and cultivating and
harrying and chopping
and thinning
and weeding
and laying by. They/stay out
there working
from sunup
till sundown/all them years.

When Victor left/for Bolton;
left for the gin/I was on needles.
He'd always come back/late. Come

back with something. Mostly/he
took his first picking
to Jackson
or Flora/ginned it

with somebody else's cotton.

Cause he never got nothing/
where he owed the man.

   10
By and by Momma sick/ask
forgiveness/for putting me

out in the world. Tell me/
the Lord done whipped her/
she ready; go home.

Auntie/say same thing;

way she treated me
was wrong. Each pain

taking her breath/mean
she reaping
what she sowed on me.
I don't hold no grudges;
tell them bygones
is bygones. Ask for His mercy;

He will touch them, too.

My chilluns/move on
   like crowder peas took
from bushes. Bro/overseas
where killings at. Long time
'tween letters/then we hear
nothing/after they drop
that bomb. Then/Bro coming

down road/two sacks; wobbling
like a young duck. Then my life/
a well-cropped field; something

hanging on every stalk
and vine
and 'tached to every root.

  11
Not long/Victor down low;
can't hardly sleep. Short
breath and coughs keep

him woke. Then his liver/bad
and he can't eat; start going
down. Tell me: soon be gone
over the river. Then I'm
holding him;
and he gone.
And I hear a tree fall
in my field. But he come
back

stand over me
a long time/don't say
nothing. Then he/gone.

Remembering/Jackson, John,
and Miss Easter, my Bible
and praying. Thanking

the Lord/putting all my burdens

in His Hands.

   Victor stayed
with me/still resting somewhere
in my heart. Forty-two years
with a man; ain't easy for him
leave/he with me though he gone.
But I keep going/cause I know

the Lord will make a way, somehow.

   12
Knowed Scootie down low/

heard her call Him. Tell
Him take life's suffering
away/ease her on home. But

two long years go by/she

still here. Tell me/her
life was dense woods.

And each day

she done cut down a bush
   pulled up a sprout
   sawed down a tree
   and dug up a stump

til all/clear.

  Then/she start

fencing in her land;

finding a plank here
and one there. Afterwhile/it

all done. She seen her way

clear; He done touched her.

Seeing her/kinda drifting/made me
feel part of myself sinking.

That thing/sucking her life away;

it start

on one breast
skip over to the other one
run down in her bones
and hop into her lungs.

She/gone and my insides ache.
Worries cloud my mind. Walking
to her grave/meant roots of my harvest
on top of the ground. And grief

can't smell the flowers.

13
Remembering/my long time;
ninety-four and more. Every
sunrise/a gift. Roses for just
living. Every midday/a hymn
for veins and bones. And evening/
soft music as the moon and
stars sing. All the days/I clap
for more. Our lives/our treasure.
What little we got/from working;
ain't been much.

We done worked/Lord knows
we have. All the rows/our
feet trailed plows down;
all the nights we sot out,
pulled up, and dug. All the
time/we sure worked. But the

land got it all; got my husband,
my third child, and my baby.
Walter/git my breakfast and
talk. Gone/the land got him.
Funeral at Mound Hood/buried
near Sixteen Sections. Ground
got him/my steps the heaviest
yet.

   14
O remembering/I lived
on the land. Home plots/
that took everything. Bore
seven chilluns and seven
grandchilluns on the dirt.

Multiplied for this earth/
there and cried and suffered
and ached and pained and
bled there; yet I live on/
cause I believe in my Lord/
trust in Him, though, sometimes
trials weigh me down.
Losing my baby/

like a ton
on my back. Done told you/faith
lifted up my feet/and hope brung
them down again. Know my Lord/is
sweet; and He is love. Sweet,
oh so sweet/He put peach scents
on my lips/every day. And I

lives on cause I know/He will
make a way/oh yes, He will make
my way, somehow

Human Rights

(for the Pontiff)

1
i did not know
that a vicar of christ
could switch sides,
that morality was relative.

the church did come
to "indians with
the conquistadors' swords."
it was genuflection

before the conquerors
or instant death.
the good hand of justice
was a conquistador's hand

and the asiento
was pontificated
so africans would know
chains and genocide.

a papal hand
signed the asiento
and rested quietly
as spanish blades

subdued "pagans"

and brought "savages"
to the "new world,"
to "civilization."

   2
i did see the vicar
pointing, with the sharpness
of steel, near hearts, as spirits
went home to ancestors

or accepted the crucifix,
didn't i? the church
came through "vicars"
of spanish conquest

while the one robed in white
folded his hands
in silence, as thousands
upon thousands received christ
or at least the sword.
the church and oppression
are old friends, aren't they?
drinking buddies, maybe?

visits when terror
spelled "indian"
wasn't the "in thing"
back then, was it?

or was it the globe
was much too much
an obstacle without
the blessing of a jet.

3

i believe it was
fidel and che who preached:
the last shall be
first wasn't it?

their teachings removed
swords from hearts
and fear dissolved
as victims joined victims

to teach the world
a new way—that
the hereafter is man
building a better world.

their blood brought
land to the landless,
and hope sprouted
among the multitudes

existing under tyrants
who keep them poor
and near death;
who keep them suffering.

the poor shall inherit
the earth (okay) or take it
with their guerrilla dances
through the times.

4

is it not ex-cathedra
for the holy jet
to descent on runways
where tyrants repress,

and the poor is not
rising up and overcoming?
is south africa too far
for a visit?

would parchman farm
provide too strenuous
a test in geography?
is lebanon too small?

tell me, father.
when you flip a coin
of morality in a oppressed
man's days,

do you get right
and wrong on both sides?
will your infallible finger
ever shake in botha's face?

in reagan's? in thatcher's?
ain't it good news
when little men
rise up, striking for freedom...?

L.A. Riot

(for America)

Kerner need not
resurrect his commission.
The verdict
is a recurring theme.
I wonder
if Dred Scott left
behind letters.
I wonder
if there are Plessy vs. Ferguson
interviews somewhere.
I wonder
if Howard has Sterling Brown's banjo
So
I can play his echo.

The niggers did it a
gain. I wonder
if Dred Scott left
behind letters.
The verdict
is a recurring theme.
I wonder
if there are Plessy vs. Ferguson
interviews somewhere.
The niggers did it a
gain. The niggers

in their heads. Let
Kerner take his rest.
The verdict
is a recurring theme.
The niggers did it a
gain. The niggers

in their heads. I wonder
if Howard has Sterling Brown's banjo.

So
I can play his echo:

ain't no need, baby.
Ain't no need, baby.

The niggers did it a
gain. Ain't no need, baby,

to be tole. The niggers

in their heads.

Three Mile Island

1
the first crack of atom's secrets
was a discovery

man understanding how
to use laws
because his reason triumphed
over nature

2
in '45
they detonated it
to end Japan's challenge to hegemony
over Asian lands

several hundred thousand
was but a small price
to save American blood
from spillage

was not too much
to end a war (after all
to save democracy

3
in the '50's
you know the Reds
were bout to overrun mankind
like huge dominoes

so they
 detonated atmospherically
to learn how bombs could kill

more efficiently

the more megatons packed in their stomachs
the better

  4
by the 60's
they had taken wild atoms
and placed them in reactors

had taken these not yet tamed
destruction genes

and placed them

  near cities
  towns and communities

so their electrical power would raise
margins of profit
though most certain to kill
with fall-outs from seepage

(if not reined properly)

  they were left

to exhale their breath of doom
over millions

5
at Three Mile Island
children are but a small price
for corporate greed
to spread

though they must live
chopped off lives
still their parents must pay

for the losses

After Reading Detained

(for Ngugi Wa Thong'o)

Not being defined
weightless as a Yoruba
without ancestors

With only consumption
and materialism
to insure my self with a number

An Afro-American

Stranger to my past
and alien in my homeland
yet a bearer of cards and cash

Not know what class
allegiance is due
because no territory

Is claim by my name
detention is absolute
since this exiled geography

Is a cell difficult
to acknowledge

—faces are doomed

To perpetual inundations
of terrors
because my jailers hire, educate, advise.

Still Malcolms come
from behind locks
to testify clarity

And all detainees
revolting against the Eagle
jump from my memory

Like sparks from a flintstone
as Cinque co-opts an Amistad
as L'Overture cradles San Domingo

As Harriet frees slaves
in midnight flights
and as David Walker says

It is better
to be dead
than an unfree slave

And thousands
unknown and heroic
resist messages chains have

Through their defiance
with John Brown at Harpers Ferry
with Yankees in a Civil War.

Bound by space
and aggregate cries
behind smiles

Alone/i sit watching days
held by a power
making compradors

Incarcerate you
where puppets from their gods
proseletyze

Yet here culture
is ground by centuries
and i hold to a blues

A spiritual
a little signifying
and a dance somewhere

Defying throbbing
crescendos of separateness
only a well-fed

Slave knows
in his cell/made visible
by reading a life.

Quilomban

(for Angela Gilliam and Abdias do Nascimento)

when your spirit
scratched fire on Palmares's breath
the voices
sang African days in a wild sky
the womb of continuity
spread from Zumbi's hands

when the Luso-vultures
came ravaging evil
your knife met throats
with Luiza's motherly power
the city you saved
laid Chico-Rei's cornerstone

bonzo/they labelled you
as their gods
came whispering, "tomorrow"
they tried to take
your ancestor core

quilomban, you have lived
through "co-colonization"
through "segregation"
through "Apartheid"
through "racial democracy"

you, the exiled root

have grown deep
for i know you
as nat turner
as sojourner truth
as harriet tubman
as denmark vessey
as frederick douglas

you, supreme abibiman
culture keeper of slaves
spread your way
over ghettoes
over favelas
over townships

let your spirit
scratch fire
on me

Grenada

1
down this alien geography of blood
this hemisphere languishing in lies

told

to hide all the genocide
the Americas mean

to those without guns

Amerindians
Africans
Toilers

all the "niggers" of space
repeatedly done in
quelled
subdued
pacified

in order for the glib illusion
of progress to pass into mythology:
Civilization, Greatness, Democracy,
Freedom...

2
i lift my time from scattering bones

this place
this shrinking void suctioning in goodness

i lift my dreams to life
and survive the roads of terror

nameless and cursed by desire
by those bent on robbing.

i rise
i rise
i rise

up through the puke and heels
of history

a flower perfuming the seasons

   3
yet the unprovoked envy of power
wants the aroma of my halo

and sends its Marines
to crush the petals of my spirits
to amputate the stems of my pride
to burn the greenness from my roots

down this alien geography of blood
this hemisphere languishing in lies

still
they tell lies
to hide all the genocide

the Americas mean

to those without guns

still
they envy the height of my uplifted palms
they despise the glow of my maturation
and send in their destroyers
to mow me down
yet
i fight and fight and fight
and rise
up through their thunder

Toi Toi

(for John O. Killens)

I take what
the sounds give
I invent
from the earth
before me. March
a thousand miles
in rhythm. In steps
to a communal fist
moving in a groove.

Toi toi is my
war cry, my
blues stepped to.
And blues is
the syringe of
my soul.

Toi
toi: the right-sized
tire for treason's neck. A committee
running Alexandra,
Nat Turner crying
pages of a new day
from memory.
The pain I reel
from my mother's bending and
keeping on in Mississippi's

magnolia whispers hushing
the curses my fathers
yelled from graves. My
grandmother's ninety-seven
years/witnessing curtains
raised and ripped down
over her name. The lynchings
in her eyes and daylight
in her hands like dough.

Toi toi/her slow steps
from my mother's grave.
Her silent trek from her baby's
burying place. Winnie's years
with Nelson behind bars.
Her defiance in "native robes".
Her war cry which hope of
unknown bards. Who count graves
in Soweto and plan tomorrow.

Toi toi is resurrection,
a dance in death's face,
steps' side Apartheid's head.

Toi toi/the mother in a place/
giving birth. My father's
life/drawn from his stillness
by my sister's grief. I
sometimes forget and say blues.
The pain. Misery. Hurt. and
abuse. Folded in tongues and
moaned out to a slow dance of
will.

Toi toi/a slow dance
down long roads, steps against
tornadoes and hurricanes.
The music/I hold my breath
to.

Toi toi down lines of steps
into bosoms of our definitions.
"Going my way, blood?" we asked
past King's assassination.

Toi
toi/the rage and dreams I danced
over burning gravel I began

toi
toing in youth and still dance
in middle age. Blues/wakes me
to creation and I move like a myth.
Epics/I climb from to my mission
along dark paths of: Hughes, Hayden,
Fuller, Neal, Danner, and Wright.

Toi toi/my will in motion
with messages I can
not tell, for they are rolled up
in generations of my blood

Composer

(for Mickey Leland)

1

He who prepares bread knows
the soul. For daily hungers are genocides.
Patches of desert spreading. Hunger.
Inheritance of African children. Swollen
bellies. Ribs on parade in mirrors of skin.
Hunger. Inheritance of African children.
Somebody stole fields of their time.
Somebody raided Africa. Took her
calendars. So stunted futures would
prosper. It was not the Sahel but the
sequel to imperialist's greed. Three out
of ten babies died in: Ethiopia,
Mozambique, and Sudan. African
children: highlight films of horror, slow
tempo mortality. Children of no flesh.
Children of deep-set eyes. Children of
Renamo. Children of war. Children of
deep rivers gone dry. Children of nobody
knows the troubles I see. Children of go
down Moses in this century. African
children. Hunger. Their inheritance.

2

Mickey. You walked trails of
skeletons: families of children strewn by
wind. Spirits restless because no grave

marks the places. You counted steps to
refugee camps where bloated bellies
reached alone. You held red-haired black
children as death gathered their faces
from this continuing generation.

You rocked children in this rite
of silence: a generation near your bosom.
You healed its appetite. African children:
nobody counts their deaths. Mickey.
You, maker of loaves, copyrighted their
suffering. For somebody needs to tell
black lives as his own. But, you, sculptor
of dough, copyrighted their suffering to
deter this new art form from encroaching
over their bones.

Mickey. You, legislator of touches,
subpoenaed hunger: the inheritance of
African children. Your fingers cross-
examined time with music. I hear it
calling dreams from brown eyes in a dark
land. I hear it calling.

Poem

(for the Blues Singers)

Poems are not places.
There are no maps for centuries
where the geography of skin
is anonymous in memory.
I am a second-handed dream
in concrete slabs of silence.
Somewhere bones speak
for my name/over fibers
of their secrets. My poems
are wanderers, meandering
in crevices between distances
and tombs. Where my voice
is bound with hammering against
the anvil of truth.

Poems are bridges, neon
reaches across worlds
where language seeks
a voice for itself. Where words
are steps up towers
of perception. I exist
in language I invent
out of ruins. Out of
the nameless sand wind
scatters as my soul.
I exist in lines of spirits.
Who gather in longings

blues singers peddle for
sweat. I exist, landless,
cropping my dreams in soil
from distances and silence
only travelers of the Middle Passage
own

Logged In My Eyes

I.
Companion
The story. Anchor
laden rover. The
blues always.
Here. After holocausts.
Laughter. A people
crying with.
Black night.
The journey. I/ramble
home/familiar
in sweet pain. I chose
joy. I stole the
fire from hail. Yeah.
A toe/heel. Rhythmic
dance of courage.
Bones/gouged out by
fingers/telling hymns.
I echo/from a child
hood of affirmations.
In a Dixie sack. No
body cares. No
body loves. Genocide
and chains. I take
by the hand. A guitar
is a witness to rivers
I have logged in my eyes.

Slaps/for

the fever I got.
Fever/when you hold me
tight. Dirt roads
to self. The old memory.
Broken parts of a dream/ I
count. As legends. Blues.
I gotta love some
one. Why not let it be you.
Said/blues. I gotta love some
one. Why not let it be you.
I gotta dream some
one. Why not let it be
you. I got pores in my soul.
Got sores on my memory.
Blues.
I reach/wisdom
in absences. Trying
to make a deal/for
the losses I can/not for
get. Blues. I may
stay back/moaning. Under
what memories drank.
Or I may leap up/in
rhythm on to/day's
face. Or I may
pound my hands/thundering
over a cross cut saw.
Chiming in tomorrows.
Blues.
I said, like I am
snake/coiled up lonely
in my dark/room. I
develop myth every day/I

dream.
Blues.
I born with/you.
Can't
get you/outta
my words. Your tongue
winds my name in palms of
your centuries.
Blues.
The morning/I dig up.
Got my future wrote
down on it/before I
even sweat rain.
Got my future wrote
down on it/before I
even sweat rain.
Got
my navel's callings
initialed on it.

Blues.
Out of stone cold
loneliness/I take the
best part of my pain.
I invent it a/gain and
a/gain. Each second I
live. Hands in/side
my pockets for their sleep.
Red clay justice/I can't
use.
Blues.
I got hard/times.
Had

them before/got them.
Every century/I roaming.
Slow
train coming/I
pulling it/with a
song.
Blues.
I wanna love you, baby.
You, my groove.
Blues.
Beats/you make in
memory.
Make me/yours.
Blues.
The same groove,
my father,
my grand
father held on.
Sun
rises in my groove.
All
ways trying to tell some
body a/bout my baby.
Blues.
You, the cherry blossom.
I/brung from Mississippi.
Round/silhouettes of a
rope.

2.
Kali
It's a low/down
a low/down bloody
shame. My history
sprawled out/on
the ground. My father's
name/bleeding red clay.
My grand/father's days
swallowed up/by mud.
I asked for Harold's lever
yester/day. To/day I gotta
look. See if my name
on the rolls. It's
a low/down, low/down
dirty shame. They keep
my humanity on empty.
Call it/equality. I
asked/for a thin dime/they
poured me/a quart of
turpentine.

Night owns a cosmos
because dragons in its hours
made it/from my tattered nerves.
I am a back/yard man.
Blues.
Scattered over acres.
Plessy
versus
Ferguson/on back
seats/in my mind.

Moaning.
Some call me:
Slave Castle Juba.
Some call me:
Jim Crowed Will.
Because/I sing blood.
Blues.
You, architect.
You, dream-myth.
You, totem pulses.
I/straighten out curves.
You wear.
I take bends
in your half/cracked smile.
Knit my
self a jumper.

Cross/roads, my formula
for destiny. Old
puzzles/striding
from bones of hours.
I all/ways grapple
with. Cross/roads,
barred gates/I gotta
open in sprints. Find
orchards under
neath pledges/ rotting in
side my breath.
The low/down hind
sight/genocide threw
shake eyes over/in cries
of my stanzas. Empty

road, blind road/where
will you push my song?
I see my father. Listen
to my grand/mother moan
her mother's chains/at
the cross/roads. Don't
know/where I live. Don't
know why I travels this way.
Where an/other possum
up in my tree.

You got no right. To
bones of time. They
tell me.
Blues.
You got no right. To the gate
way/eye of tongues.
The cross
roads beckoning.
Lazarus ascents. From
pits of slave
ships. From
terrored anguish in the Middle
Passage's rib cages.
You got no right/longing.
Ain't
no law/uphold dreams.
They tell me.
Blues.
You, like a stone tumbling
down a hill.
They tell me.

Blues.
Every
time you/open your mouth.
Some
thing bad/chunked outta it.
They tell me.
Blues.

You
got blood gurgling/rattles
under your tongue. When
you
speak/bloody birds fly/outta
your lungs.
To beats of songs and
hand
claps from air.
They tell me.
Blues.
You got no right/with
hinges on your tongue.
So

memory can climb up veins
in your throat/over
a hundred bleeding miles.
Got
no right/make pages
you
writing on/howl and stomp
they feet.
When

the sweet words hit them.
They tell me.
Blues.

It's a low down, a low
down dirty shame.
Blues.
Way
they drink my blood.
Then
say ain't no/thing
in my mind.
Low/down,
low/down dirty shame.
Blues.
Way
they drink my blood.
Then
swear ain't no/thing
good/even been mine.
Say
fruits feeding culture
from their origins.
While
pushing my sound
under/ground.
Way
I sing the blues on paper/I
swear it's a crime.
My
clothes dirty and ragged.
And I

ain't got one scarce dime.
They tell me.
Blues.
You got no right/put
shame on your name.
They tell me.
Blues.
Your time/a dog
gone shame.
Your history/a crying
shame. And you/dare
wait at the cross
roads. Let
memory spread this/out
to ages.
It's a shame, it's
a shame.
Way
they treated poor me.
Blues.

Another Mule Muddy Waters

Another mule kicking
I say another mule
kicking moans/ in my face
Mississippi's sorrows

Aching with deltas
year long hopes wash
muddy/scattered by dread
visions of death holds

Above daylight/backs tender
from bending over rows and rows
of barren dreams
stalks are haunting

Against grey skies wiping
tears with damp clouds
greedily smeared about
timeless eyes

Mississippi legends
thrown above hollers
another mule, another mule,

The crumbling city
walls falling on my futures

Ritual

(for Daniel Wideman)

Some poets
got gyms
for their words.
And I
gotta take my lines
to the hoop
on gravel.

Blues.

Song

as the high
way I
hit.

Words

that reach out
like arms. Grabbing
for something
I
can hold on
to.

Pal of
the no
body in my
loneliness.

Tales
who know
their way
home.

Sun
pilot lights
for my stove.
Moon
light bulbs
in my frigidaire.

A
fitness
test
for the
soul.

Blues

Mingus: Watchman of Hours

(for Jacob Wideman)

   You
could cut
around midnights
at noon. Hind
the glare of a great
smile somewhere
in Mississippi.
Between "baby" and
a long memory soaked
in garlic syrup. Break

into the open field of
be-bop, shifting strides,
to avoid Max Roach
or Art Blakely
in the flats, change
direction to barrel
over axmen near sunsets
in the West. Ornette,
Albert, Pharaoh, and
Archie. Free
to slide a hegemony of

moods

  into the end zone.

You
can get through
to African gods
when the lines are

busy

Blues/Scapes

1
Night got a pearl
handle. Chambers tensions with
in a mean circle, I can
not break. A wreath of hollers
lags a/round my navel. Laments gate
ways in my sleep. A battle
ground/I wake up. Ready/for
distances.

2
Old man. Sediment in
side the hieroglyphs of knots,
puffy veins, and geometric
wrinkles on his face. A blues
tradition I can
see. Gashes a
cross a half mile his
countenance/bending
his spirit. One third the after
noons/mules shit
in his eyes. Cussed him
out/with tail lashes. I
hear logged on snake-eyed
knees. At bucket-a-blood
rites. Where you gotta roll
to stay in the fold.

3
Old fenced in moon/ray
Falling through/grips.
Retired planks once
had. The blues/I'd rise
to. Day/break calling
field-handed-morning. Pick
cotton, pull corn. Might
find a grain. Pick cotton, pull
corn. Get a bushel of pain
in the end.
Talk. The song/longing.
Are you ready? For the
lost whistle. I tell you I
tell you. Every century/I
have the blues. If you
see me coming/my daddy
done paid my dues.
Memory/an allegory of
the trump cards/I
lost. "If you ain't gon
git it on/take your tired
rump home."*

4
Stormy minutes/all
ways dogging my time.
Bad whisky/popping tnt.
The hole. Last place/troubles
climbing over my blues.
A cup of soot in my eyes,
a fire/place burn on my knees,
but my back at the north pole.

Thunder/claps all
ways inching in my hours.
Some pounding history
lets holes in my ease.

5

The only sorghum/I got.
Flows bitter. The last drop.
Slow. The indebted farmer's
cries. Own a corner in my essence, a plot
where they
cultivate wringing hands.
To wipe sorrows from eyes.
I got the-everything-gone
wrong-blues. I am scared
to see the sun rise. Some
body might have a rope/my neck's
size. I got the-bare-boned-
outdoors-blues. Gotta pay
the drought/for not bringing
rain. Can't get near a shower/it
might collect its due/with my bloody pain.

6

Pushed down, broke down/every
day. Get up/swinging the
blues. Keeping time
with an ancestral rhyme.
Slop hogs, feed chickens
corn. Said I slop hogs, feed
chickens corn. Been humping
since the day I born. The
I-can't-get-away-blues/I got.

Burdens. My daddy/not there
at my birth. Said my daddy/he
hit and run. My granddaddy took
his place. I look in the mirror, it
in so much pain/I can't recognize
my own face.

7

The I-maybe-lost-in-the-lonely-
hole-in-the-ground-blues/I got.
Unlived dreams my daddy left/rot out
side my reach. Send cold funk
from the maggots's curses
to my eyes. And I cry/bitterness
in/to the image/debts and Jim
Crow carved from my sweat.
The call me the-getting-it-on
man cause that/my last name.
I try so hard to tell my history
the page breaks out in a flame.

8

Night train gone/when I get
up, day train late/coming by.
Night train gone/when I get
up, day train late/coming by.
Mississippi drinks so much/my
blood I kin lay down and die.
New ground I cleared out/covered
back over with trees. New ground
I cleared out/covered back over
with trees. Mississippi get every
thing I got/too damn mean to say

please. But long time ago I thought
I had left this hell. But long time
ago I thought I had left this hell. So
if magnolia/the only flowers you got, Lord
knows, I just don't wanna smell.

Keyman

(for Son Seals)

Brigadier shouter
in your cross cut assurance.
A list of wood
to saw in your gestures.
A marquee of screams
swings
between your cries and
your smile.
Where arias of shadows
ascend from week-ends.
A bare footed spirit
dances. And
you
open Saturday night
lids with frowns. And
be
come the second coming of
a name: an orphic bottomland
furrowed by hollers.
I-am-down-and-out
is a recurring visitor
you
evict with a forty-four
loaded with moons.
Even
in your mildewed laughter
despair is an endangered species

you
register for annihilation.

In this
house, out of pain
where you stop slow rain inside.

With fossils from
your guitar's vaccinations

A Hundred Miles Inside

They say blues is a feeling
troubled like a rising tide.
They say blues is a feeling
troubled like a rising tide.

I believe it is my little song
I pull from a hundred miles inside.

They tell me it's better to walk
when a stranger offers you a ride.
They tell me it's better to walk
when a stranger offers you a ride.

Might wanna kidnap your little song
you pull from a hundred miles inside.

I'm told that pain is on the prowl
I ain't go nowhere to hide.
I'm told that pain is on the prowl
I ain't got nowhere to hide.

I just put it in my little song
I pull from a hundred miles inside.

They say blues is a feeling
troubled like a rising tide.

They say blues is a feeling
troubled like a rising tide.

I believe it's my little song
I pull from a hundred miles inside.

Stitchings

(for Honeyboy Edwards)

Wardrobe of memory.
History with
out a tie. Or
white shirt. A mis-matched
collage of limited
engagement.

Sponsored
by a one-eyed seamstress
from backseats of years
kept inside calendars
women sequester
in folded hands.
Tailor, a singer,
monitor of spirits,
talks his designs.
His shouts
before daybreak
forecast days I
wear. A titular
servant, handless and legless.
Gambles against fire
with his eyes and
winnings echoed
across chasms
in eternity. Are
styles I swear
before

Mister Hard Times

Went to the store to get myself a coke
they sell it only by the glass
Went to the store to get myself a coke
they sell it only by the glass

Can't get no satisfaction
till my lowdown blues pass.

Ask the bartender for a drink
a shot of Beefeater gin
Ask the bartender for a drink
A shot of Beefeater gin

He say I ain't got nothing
My days held together by a safety pin.

Mister hard time, Mister hard times,
dressed in your Calvin Klein.
Mister hard times, Mister hard times,
dressed in your Calvin Klein.

Must think you are a millionaire
don't have to pay the hard time fine.

So bad here I seen prayer thumb a ride.
So bad here I seen prayer thumb a ride.
And luck working overtime
and hoboing on the side.

It's so hard when my baby quit me
Sued her for part of my hurt
It's so hard when my baby quit me
Sued her for part of my hurt.

Judge say let's make things equal
Cuz you both specialize in dirt.

Mister hard times, Mister hard times,
dressed in your Calvin Klein.
Mister hard times, Mister hard times
dressed in your Calvin Klein.

Must think you are a millionaire
don't have to pay the hard time fine.

Went to the store to get my self a coke
they sell it only by the glass.
Went to the store to get myself a coke
they sell it only by the glass.

Can't find no satisfaction
till my lowdown blues pass.

Music/Calling

Some/body, long gone,
waits to auction off
pain. They bid'em
in blues festivals.

Billy returns. The old
man behind his breath
sighs. Pulls. Pulls.
That's why the blues paid
my fare. Going. Going.
To ask the wind for a
slice of please. Some
times I cry a laughter/I
got to keep under burdens.
I in/herited from a moaning
relative who jumped over
board in/to legend.

Mister Lost Love. Got
keys to Billy's hands. He
pays tribute to moons. Crying
a ring of generations. Ring of
griots. Music/calling

Homeland

Homeland

Here. I wander
among myths.
Where scars are
metaphors up
graded by will.
A
puzzle of fragmented
bits of soul.
America,
the passage;
riddle with a language
I
invent.
Where memory
is a cellblock;
sleep, a dubious
invitation. And
dream is a phalanx
with blues as the
pediatrician of
the spirit. I
always peddle
in dust, suspended.
Maneuvering
within the
passage. Hoping
for gospel,
my delivery nurse,
taleteller of

handclaps and dance.
Near
home of the laser
surgeon,
jazz.
Where a spiritual
swings
loas between galaxies of
eyesight.

I'm a soul fixer.
I specialize in hope
repair

Kimberley

(for Albie Sachs)

Here.

There are women

who are close relatives
to head
rags. And
mops. And
brooms.

Like the Mississippi.
I know.

And cleanings.

Like the American dream.

My mother.

Lived.

Galeshewe

(for David Theys)

I know not kings.
But
Prosser, Vessey, and
Turner. Who made
my name a freed wing.

And
you expired a martyr
in royalty.
For soil and
dreams.

I
come to your thousands of
names where
your
crown is a silhouette of graffiti:

Amandla!
Freedom Square.
Long Live SACP.
Tambo 403.
Mandela Square.
Long Live ANC.
Amandla!

Your

squatter camps
are dynamites
loaded with hopes.
Their
mother is struggle.

I know
your unpaved streets and
laughter. Your impromptu
concerts in kitchens.

Your
Pentacostal Will of the Holy Ghost
snake dancing across yards and roads;
wheels of prayers calling on High.
I know.

Your
masks of slowness,
ease, and idleness.
I
know in Mississippi with
in me where trees
bear `strange fruits'.

Galeshewe.
There is a veil
over your face and
I live behind it.
In tabernacles of urban decay
where my brothers kill
their own images
who are strangers to them.

Where they strike like cobras
because love is a foreigner.

Your
squatters,
a festival of sharecroppers
in my memory,
know the earth.

They
trudge from the grave
yard from toilets.
Go
there for their water.
At least,
Apartheid provides
for the dead.

And
your spirit remains a
spring here in

this place
I know.

Galeshewe

Orange Free State

(for Lionel Beukes)

Rows and rows and rows.

Match
box shacks. Perhaps,
your shot
gun is not architecture.

But,
your dark faces
wandering paths.
Your
miles and miles and miles of
wealth. Reflect
the Mississippi Delta
with ored-veins.

Your
blacks huddled
at the cross
roads must have
a Robert Johnson or
Bessie Smith
to moan destinies
from flooded overtures.

Some
how. Your land

scapes are familiar.

I have been here.
In easy rhythms of
black women, some
thing balanced
on their heads, a hymn
tucked beneath silenced
lips. For a rainy day.

I have been here.
In slow deaths in eyes of
black men with bottles. Empty
pockets and terror sending them
to long nights and nights.
Wandering to no
where from hungers.

Your
music is mine. Manifolded rhythms
interpreted anew. Each second,
stretched out, rolled into patches of leather,
personal styles, worn as melody. Your
music is mine in battles
with stagnant waters. Where improvised rivers
ascent genius to crush banks of a place
without permits to govern.

Your
music is mine

Township

(for the Civics)

O nobody nobody.
O nobody nobody knows.
O nobody nobody knows.
O nobody nobody.

Place of rest.
Martin L. King, Jr.
sends you amandlas
from his agape-laden dream.

Phomolong.

Pushed into shadows
by gold fields.
Your yards
five deep
with houses.
Each with five
families.
Your streets
unpaved.
My drug addicts
send you aborted
greetings
with needle marks and
crack killings
for turf.

There
is defiance in the mokgibo of your children.
There
is affirmation in the tolobonya of your children.

Your
squatter camps huddled
to defy genocide.
Nat Turner sends
you a prophecy: I will be
with you in your hour of
birth.

Phomlong.

You,
land of black, green and gold.
You,
land of children a-plenty.
Land of mokgibo.
Land of tolobonya.
Land of amandlas.
May God Bless the Child That
Got Its Own
is a maintenance worker
inside your dreams.

Your marshals
welcome me with salutes.
Your daughters
embrace me with songs.
Land of rest.

My black panthers
are your cousins.

Kingdom of
beautiful dark faces.
Eyes
with smiles.
I bring the Mississippi blues
to your hardships.
I
bring spirituals
to your longings.
For my underclass
is blood of your blood.

I
bring my lynch rope
as a signature for your terrors.

Phomolong.

Land of Mokgibo.
Land of tolobonya.
Land of amandlas.

Land of rest.

Thaba Nchu

You
call me from your chair of
riveting nights. A fire
place by your spirit.
Mountain of
songs where languages gather.
You
call me.

Near
your dark feet they hitch teams
in towns; a cryptic reminder of
my grandfather's Saturdays
in Mississippi. His week
done and meal and sugar
needed for another. His week
done and he gone to Bolton or
Clinton til long after darkness.

Crescent beauty of your landscapes
bearing rich dark bosoms. Where

cassava or melon or okra
or yam or bean or cabbage
could build nations around
your toes.

Black Mountain.
Black Mountain.

Conspirator of awe
in openness of widening plains.
Inventor of sources
on rolling hills.
You
call me.

Your
lithographs of shadows,
like wings of a condor,
devour the air with solitudes.

Windows
in pauses of your ascent
choreograph months in my past.

And ancestry in my pen
nods its appreciation.

The
throng I see, half-stepping,
wages of debts on heads,
half-stepping a slow-drag
with distance under vile heat.
They
are cotton pickers in my childhood
hoping for rain.
They
are youth in my city
stalking for murder.
The
half-step, I see

is a dirge waltz or
a war dance of survival.

There
under your dusk glances:
Solomon Mahlangu elementary and
Chief Moroka high.

Black Mountain.
Black Mountain.

Tell me.

Why
bend your head
down to your knees
for the

sun

Weaver

(for Kim Ngqawana)

Your
spiralled agony.
Your
remembered speech.
Marches
in your tones.
How
did you
get from here
to Harlem and
back on a
Trane?
Where I hold
reservations on your Express Distanced Voyager.
Over
the shadows I saw
darting
through blackness
in Alexandra.
Darting
through nights and
nights.
I know.
The signatures of pain
scribbled on wind.
I have
known in runawayed flights

from chains and
changed names.
The
Sometimes I Feel Like A Motherless Child
fisted cries.
I know.

You
voyaged from lynch ropes
to the sprawling metaphors of
Soweto.
Nights and
nights.
The
boy shot in the head on my block.
You
play his cry in longings
where the eclipses of your rhythms.

Pummel
horrors outside the door of

my mind

Johannesburg

(for Zwelakhe Sisulu)

Every breath you take
is a lyric.

1
All the loneliness in
side.

Pothole in memory. Cloudy
universe of bricks. I
battle for aromas I left in
side spaces on land.
Cosmos without weather reports
for hearts. I know you.
Place of fragments.
Where silences are classified ads
in ears. Who recruit
survivors. Where loneliness
plays mama peg on faces
with unknown touches.
Where biographies of
loved ones are mimeographed
on darting shadows.
Place blues come,
where the songs without shoes
congregate. Where tales
which give titles to miles of
suffering toted in a day,

gather. Where every step
is a riff, an adjoinment of
whips. Where wounds gather
for tea. Where a hornman
handcuffs the wilderness
blindfolded. And a trumpeter,
whose every gesture is a song,
announces calendars of hard times
behind smoke from greyhound
stones speeding along boulevards of
angry hands.
Like New York, you are host of
the First Family of strangers.
As harbinger of openings,
a trumpeter says: never repeat
a command but once and live.
And a keyboard picks
new agendas as an afterthought.
Moans deaf blood to sequences
in tablets he opens. Moans
lineage of dreams on parole.
Felons with breathing spaces
between Abdullah's fingers.
Moans purple eyes to clearings
near shoulders of the drum.
Where the melody on deck
sits crosslegged on crystal
darkness he closed in envelopes of
beats.

2
All the memories in
side.

The maids, heads
wrapped with legend.
Nurse fires and murmur
against light which flickers in
side parks. Exchange
sisterly riffs beneath a night
which knows last cries of
daughters and sons. Going
one more mile, one more mile
for a place. Going
one more mile. With their gift of
standing up shouting time
people keep in
side legends bullets can
not touch. My eyes search
among shadows and smoke and
murmurs for my mother's spirit.

I know the Mississippi earth
is not strong enough to
hold it.

3
All the places in
side.

Johannesburg.
Johannesburg.
I hear.
       The distancing of steps
accelerating on your streets.
I hear epics I know.
Allegoric dances of

a people who will not
crumble. Who accept
loneliness with blood
spilled in anonymity.
Not knowing
whose throat is slit.
Anonymity. A black hole.
For children
who communicate with sign languages of
knives. Children
whose places were swallowed
by piranhas.

Wanderers.

The place they make the place
they left. Your smile littered
with bodies. A Harlem far a
way in a dream. Labyrinths of
caverns inviting blood.
Skulls lounge
on asterisks of unsolved murders.
Crossroads
where spirit got off
at wrong depots.
Obituaries without names
queued at the lost and found.
A Harlem
Hughes' lines mapped
in Simple epics of tired feet.
Some just be tales
with blisters on them.
A black Manhattan

in Africa. Quick
deaths bargaining
with flesh. All I remembered
about selves I buried.
I find here. Distance and
curses competing in nights.
Layered terrors unfolding
with each step. In memory,
the wagon your children
picked as voyager rattles
the melody of my solo.
The Homeless Quintet
commissioned for casseroleless
urban diets.

History is an island
which floats. The

drummer fishes and catches
it. Max Roach beats breakfast and
Bird orders omelets; Dizzy wants
his grits.

   4
Out of a sharp blade
a photograph of a century's lungs
crying interns for unborn hymns
ahead.

An inventory of names
I have longed four hundred
years. Flattened by under
brush. Your soul, laminated

tiers of metal. Johannesburg.
Where your graphite eyes
serve jury duty at midnight.
Casting
judgments. The trumpeter swallows
after his embouchure declines
silence iron guardians
require for order. Lets
the bassist intercede
with rhythms whores
on your corners anoint
one another bitches.
The domain of spirit
is my landscape. He says.
Johannesburg. You,
the city I find myself
an alien out
law. The trumpeter appeals
for my identity. For
liberation of my name. Calls
for a session where the guitarist
eats statistics condemning me
with criminal profiles. And
the saxman makes stew
from screams renting rooms
from kitchenettes of the ground.
I live the here
say. Your infidel brightness
prolongs in its intervals of
attempts to evict shadows.
Who occupy wired braids of
your bobbing skyline.

If your walls were removed
they could build three
cities. Bars on your doors
could support bridges
across every chasm
on Africa's broad face.
Your anatomy contains
symbols I interpret
my America with. Here.
I am told your Air Force
places bars on the sky
after each sunset to keep
darkness from overtaking
the mother light. I wonder
if your locks have forms
for the interior of
your houses to apply for
a furlough. Johannesburg.
They say each breath
in Soweto is a heartbeat
in you. And Alexandra
is your appropriate shoe
size. You dance if it
doesn't ask you to sit
in stillness. I ask
if music has hands
for something touched me
last night; only Hugh's sounds
were there.

5

Deep rivers I want to say
you are the home I got

over yonder. Deep rivers.
Deep rivers, I say,
because you are the morning
I find across a long journey
on a hobby horse going
round and round. Your
sadness is a fossil in flesh.
You are my home over yonder
in canebrakes. You are
my home over yonder in swamps.
You are my home over yonder
on Parchman Farm. You are
my home over yonder in cotton
fields. You are my home
over yonder in unemployment
lines. You are my home
over yonder in homeless
wanderings.

Museums in eyes I know.
The gallows there, I know, too.
If I deny part of my reflection
in the winds where your high beams of laughter cradle
    my cries. I cannot
rest. Strolls across your avenues
are medicinal. The silhouette
meshed in darkness is your poet.

Here where dance is a napkin of
greatness. As he bobs and weaves
through languages. Days are in custody
but he raises bail high as a guerrilla's

vision and wide as hoecakes
in a deacon's hallelujahs. Raises
bail as he bobs and weaves
through languages.

6
Your cavalcade of
languages in aerobic quizzes
against nights. Descend
on choruses of
silence where spaces of
blues are eaten
by furors of rhythm.
Somewhere
distilled arias
from briars I remember.
Appear
in Xhosa clicks
underneath a strangeness
cities prefer.
In this far away
sanctuary of concrete and
desires. SeTswana and
Zulu duke it
out on background of a
prayer whose solo
is dried blood
on corners. Near
the palace Malcolm X
emerges Big Red
with black, green and
gold insulation
beneath his skin.

Near tenements
Baldwin's ghost searches
for memories Codessa here
will release in cassettes of
spirit the Spear anointed
over porridge of dreams
I hear Mandela copyrighted
at Robben Island University
where paths to this birth
rehearsal, your crisscrossing
veins of rock, are mapped.
Where cartographers of sound
major in precisions of
spears on these bricks
knitted by years of enlarged
fangs and dust.

Your poet roams perimeters of
your eyes with pigeons
in his hands to forewarn
travellers of the Mountain's
recalcitrance which conjures to house
spirits it kidnaps. To
chain their souls
before arrival at your hard
meandering tentacles.
Who rustle goodness
like Jesse James or an
Apartheid express rider.
Highwaymen of avarice and
capital toned halos greased
on their foreheads. Your

speech owns shoulders of
darkness where your poet
weaves patterns for others
to negotiate hillsides of
genocides where I saw
ghosts of children huddled
around fires in parks.

Calling for names poverty
sponsors for concerts and
where their ribs
are stringed instruments
in an orchestra. Their
ancestral dreams are
beheaded when they are
played. Zim Ncqwana
washes his sax in their
memory. Extends invitations
to needs.

Noise in your corridors
is an agency where I file
for aid. To purchase my claim
to stand on land I
have never touched before.
To reprint songs I
remember from coal oil winters
among shadows of the plantation
I grew up on. Veils cast
over my dreams I remove
with a raised fist and lyrics
I follow with steps of toi toi
accompanying. Here my tears

long for rugs but you insist
on tin stools for their comfort.

   7

Footprints of spirits
      stop here.
      Perplexed as an octopus
on skates.

This Market Equinox
dissolves facades in glasses
black and white hands
converse. Where hopes
are returned parcel post.
The graffiti bullets imprint
on chests is sheet music
for Civic workers. Here.
Where any A-Train I take
from memory finds axles of
a combi to carry me
to the future. A sandwich of
rhythms reside where anchors of
cold feet unpack my suitcase.
At this station where songs
are helpers of dreams
without tickets.

Strangeness is a timepiece,
a crafted Bulova of rapid
heartbeats, an alarm of screams
highlighted alone. Where the train
I ride/I ride all night long.
Into a trumpet conducting surveys

among bones.

The valley of my mind
learned its ABCs between
riffs. Hornmen. Hornmen.
Name paths your streets
omits, Johannesburg. Burial
is a revival, a beginning of
handclaps against steel.

Monk thinks chordal hopscotch
with Mingus at midnight. Round
bout eruptions of possibility.
Have you ever heard a hiccup
in a stone's throat whipped
by music. Saturday nights
balled in memory. Sawdust
on pallets of tongues to catch
blood falling falling down
like gospel pain. Evangelical hurt
spread under auspices of good news
fingers preach on air. And
a Summit of Horns telling
weird tales. Old Man river
in my father veins as ballads
on tenor excursions with anecdotes.
Baptismal vows of my grandmother
as short thrusts a trumpet makes,
retracts as slurs. Cadences
as linoleum on sand, to ease
steps over darkness. Do you
know about tunnels made
by whispers.

8

Your august band of thugs
accepts my alien status;
for I come without a union
card. Precisely chiseled
as a photograph who refuses
to fade. Ancestor as curvature of
history. Burning. Burning
on installment plans.
Where blues is foodstuff of
loneliness. A smorgasbord of
feelings. One man's yield of
hurt picked by necessity.
One woman's boundary of
fruits harvested by longings.
Set on tables where your distance
and hardness join me. Dessert
is a basket of echoes dueling
with wet sticks.

9

Down these avenues.
A swelling in alto volume.
As Cannonball adlibs
surgery for a Bird's
appendix. Where I want
to pata pata someone miles
away from Miriam's voice.
Down these avenues. A
guitar knows so well.
Where I come duze someone
behind Letta's closing of

phrases into lagoons of
laughter she quiets. Down
these streets. I want to
pata pata skeletons of
dreams I lost on my way.

Johannesburg.
Johannesburg.

You,
with galvanized thongs of adventurers,
like termites.
tilt creation.

Have you ever heard
hiccups in stones's throats
whipped by music. A silence of
abundance. A barrel rich
in distances and spaces. For
solos whispered with veils
weepers throw to lowering boxes.
You,
city of tomorrow's dreams.
You,
beggar of creativity.
Have you ever had the blues.

You,
city of I wish. Music inside
resin dripping in falling blood.

Words
climbing ladders from battlefields.

Lesego. Poet of breezes
throwing bricks through windows.
His polling places of lineages.
Have you ever had the blues.

Keorapetse's eyes are catchers
in the rye. His images muddier
than the Mississippi river
he crosses to bring King
Mandela's wisdom in cross
referenced boogaloo-toi toi
gaits. Pharaoh makes him
perform.

You,
city where I unpack my matchbox
to deposit all I own in your palms
which ring like steel lordy lordy.

Poet of earth, black soil
dripping from his mouth.
Scars on skin of air
he breathes imaging
his journeys. Hard rocks
as mirrors. One man, one rope
as democracy's gift. He snares
Lesego's truth in his eyes. Then
brushes his teeth with runaway
whirlwinds he chains for the trip
back to Masekela's Plantain.
Where hopes graze on savannahs
near an arched back. Way from
his plutonium lips who decree

melons on violins

Johannesburg.
Johannesburg.

A trumpeter. Triumph of
fallen tears on his face.

A resurrection of bent
backs. Knees accustomed
to benchmarked possessions.
Here. Where my skin attracts
cruise missiles with unknown
addresses and I remember
Emmett Till or a boy shot
on the West Bank or backs
bullets prefer in Sharpeville
or Soweto or Alexandra. Here
in this launching place of hieroglyphics
your vendors tell me there are used
dream shops.

Where I unpack my matchbox
to deposit all I own in your palms.
Which ring like steel lordy lordy.
Ring like cold steel, lord.

   10
The Holiness of raised
fists with stones redeems
more territory than
smart bombs. Here at
the corner of Oppenheimer power and

shoeless wanderers. Spirits of
your children come here.
To protest. To defy. To
liberate. Like SNCCED songs of
my land. They legislate
the pace of marching feet.

Their shadows silhouetted
against a sun rising in eyes of
your poets, like a toi toi
in slow motion or some dusty
recollections of Motown
on parade or some wolf-like
taildragger walking
all the way from Dallas, Texas
with Sumlin lassoing his voice
with rhythms from the river's
many crypts. Slowdragging planets
in miniature; a shadow silhouetted
against Nkosi Sikelele in a skit;
explosions perform as invitations
for Arrogant Ones to find
bargaining tables.

      Johannesburg.
Johannesburg.

Your crossroads
draw blueprints for the next
century. Towards what prophecy
will the feet turn. What lyrics
will emerge from echoes of stone
thrower's scripts. Which roads

will Masekela's music take for
the dances.

Mutiny of cowardice
is normal along crevices of
your skin where I live
in tenements of silences.

Two months rent overdue.
I am a blues man just
as blues as I can be.
I have dominion over empty
lots. Empty glasses. Empty
eyes in skulls. Empty
bottles of dreams. Empty
ballots of power. And empty
echoes from heaven. Your
poet is an architect of
silences. Creates names
on bones lost under water.
In sewerages. Rivers.

Johannesburg.
Johannesburg.

This bitterness I drink
in America. It's cup
I find here. Offered by gaps
between teeth of alignment
and I drink again. For I
do as your poet says: lift
every cup in celebration.
Here, too, I celebrate.

With the affirming ear and
eye. Bygones I claim as
dependents because the blues
in you is the blues in me.
The orphaned memory I take
is celibate. Yet I cry
descendants from the Self.
Because the blues in you
is the blues in me.

City
of competing nights. Where my longings
find their homes.
Place
where heaven's skirmishes
spill over into my sleep.
Land
of angels wearing do-rags.
City
of magic symbols. Music.
Music. Music. Sweet
music everywhere.

Johannesburg.
Johannesburg.
Exile is a hallucinogen
that whistles. Three
hundred years of exile
is a quintet. Trumpet.
Alto. Bass. Drum. Tenor.
Music. Music. Music.
Sweet music everywhere
inside my skull. Music.

City
of competing nights. Myths
in battle gear of sounds.
A concert of steps. Sweet
music everywhere. My mind
is a hectacomb. And you,
the negative. Johannesburg.
Your
vendors hustle weekends
on the black market.
Master horologists.

While
in Yeoville your poet
records his places and
      bloodstains on his long name.
His souvenirs of lineage
he exhibits on languages of
his eyes. A fist and a dance
there refusing introductions.

Danger is vitamin C
for the spirit. Mzwakhe
says. I sell by pound
or bottle or one by one.
I live here near threats.

Cold Steel Mountain.
Cold Steel Mountain.

It performs autopsies
on dreams. It's teeth

are surgical implements.
Can't you hear it chewing,
grinding fibers. Can't
you hear it grinding,
chewing fibers. Black
night, black night falling
falling down like rain.

Kippie's estuary. We
meet there. Mzwakhe
says. Kippie's estuary
where music is a wave
repeating itself. A
continuous song I know.

A place where the present
is dangerous whether
the clouds clear or not.
Your poet says. The red
song of our blood gives
power to deal with
this mountain. I count
my years by the number of
cataracts I pull from
my eyes on the road. Where
bloodstains are special
geographies to me. On the long
road in exile I remember
wells. I remember water
in the desert of the chaos
I meet. Where the present
is a dangerous place to live
even here at Kippie's estuary

where music is a wave repeating
itself a million times.

11
I ask if this place.
This topography graced by songs.
If these avenues paved by vomit and
blood shed in honor of thieves.
I ask, Johannesburg, if your streets
know my name. For I have come back
removed four hundred years. I have
come back though I departed
Africa's western windows.
I ask, Johannesburg, if your streets
know my name.

The Response:

Cold Steel Mountain.
Cold Steel Mountain.

It eats longings. Kidnaps
spirits. Lunches on hopes.
Spits out bones of souls
down from its heights. Its saliva.
It spreads over its body
to lube it. It's greasy, you slide
back down if you try to climb it.
So high you can't go
over it. So deep you can't
go under it. So wide
you can't go around it.

Got every dream you bring
in your heart. Got every
longing you bring in your feelings.
Got every hope you bring
in your bones. Got ancestors's
lore. Got cries of dying children.
Got spirits of shebeen-headed
men. Got spirits of corner-
dressed women. Got my soul.
Got all the names I remember
locked up in its metal veins.

Cold Steel Mountain.
Cold Steel Mountain.

It the path you must take.
So high. So deep.
So wide. So solid.
So greasy. How you gonna
walk Cold Steel Mountain.

How can I find it.
It ain't never been seen.
How can I walk it.
Screams are lanterns.
Screams are lanterns.
Screams are lanterns.

But it snacks on screams
and holler. And moans
and groans are its appetizers.

It carries things on its head;

it's a woman
Nothing inside but hardness;
it's a man.
When it's mad words
cut like razors;
it's a woman.
When you need something
it in its pockets and gone;
it's a man.

Cold Steel Mountain.
Cold Steel Mountain.

Barbara says I will
stick it with my hat pin.
It might be a pimple or
a balloon. Langa says
I will blow it. It might
be tenderness of blood or
a bubble. Wally says
I will box it. It might
be a tough tale. We can't
go over it. We can't go
under it. We can't go
round it. We can't go
through it. Vusi sings.
Why not take a taxi. Njabulo
says. They go everywhere.
They can't climb greased
steel. Mafika says. How
do you know we ain't
horizontal to it. Nadine
says. Let's take a taxi.

Let's take a taxi.
Let's take a taxi.
Let's take a taxi.

Swing, swing low sweet
pata pata.
Swing, swing low sweet
pata pata.
A combi for to carry me home.

Swing, swing low sweet
pata pata.
Swing, swing low sweet
pata pata.
A combi for to carry me home.

Lord, Sweet Lord.
And I wonder if my mother's uniform
in heaven is a headrag.

Swing, swing low sweet
pata pata.

glossary of
South African
terms and
names here
(2pp)

Sterling Plumpp was born in Mississippi in 1940. He is the editor of *Somehow We Survive,* an anthology of South African writing. His collection of poems *The Mojo Hands Call, I Must Go* won the Carl Sandburg Award for poetry in 1983. His 1989 collection, *Blues: The Story Always Untold,* received wide critical acclaim. He resides in Chicago where he is an Associate Professor of African-American studies at the University of Illinois-Chicago.

Poetry in Chicago
poetry across the nation & in the world
vitality of poetry.
zen study of poetry
students